GATHER

OCTAVIA RAHEEM

ISBN: 9798621791155

www.octaviaraheem.com

GATH·ER
/ˈɡaT͟Hər/

noun
    part of a garment that is drawn in or pulled together

verb
    Assemble, accumulate

Bring together from scattered places. Draw in.
Come together.
Get together.

For Karen M. Mason
Your question, "So, what are you waiting for?"
It gathered me.

INTRODUCTION

I was four years old and in love with reading when I realized the words on a page, those small curved black-bodied things were scribbled together and created by someone.

When I realized humans could create books, I wanted to be a human who did that.

I grew up hungry, dusty, and trailer house poor. Still, I'd take my last coins, toss them into wishing fountains, and pray, *"God, pretty please let me make books."*

"You can't eat stories for dinner and grow meat on your bones." "Get your education and get you a good job with insurance." Despite my unrivaled love for reading and writing, I internalized these messages from my family and the world around me. In fear and hunger, these messages became the ones that created my reality instead of the poems and musings I dreamed up.

Does everything have to be about "bread?" When your Ancestors and mama 'nem have survived off less than crumbs, the answer has been yes for many generations.

That *yes* owned me. That *yes* owned us.

So, I jumped into that wishing fountain and snatched all of my pennies back. I pushed "writer" into a safe corner within me where she wouldn't be touched by a world that would ravish her, including my own mind.

All these years later and after feeding myself many things that never left me full, I am remembering my first love.

Remembering what is real to me is the gift of my yoga and meditation practice and the awakening I have experienced within it.

My practice allows me to remember what I feel like beneath my surface level, that level that I allow the world to see. Through devotion, my practice has softened and opened the tough and hidden cords around my heart and unraveled a holy thread of memory and truth.

The deep-eyed Black girl who loved the sound and feel of words on her tongue more than the sour taste of green apple Now and Later candy or the small beads of pure sugar in the first few chews of Bubble Yum gum, and my Cabbage Patch doll, Annie. That little country girl with imagination bigger than ancient oak trees, that me, is awake and present.

I no longer need writing to yield "surance," as my granny would say. It's about more than "bread." It's salvation and soul food.

I only need to assure my inner four-year-old that she is worth the effort and offering.

Writing allows me to practice imperfection. Through practicing imperfection, I am able to access the wild beauty of my humanity in a deeper way. In the words of Outkast, "Now that's liberation."

I choose to show up to my altar (my desk) with devotion each day. I choose to sit there and listen until I hear that pigtailed child who was brave enough to toss away pennies on a wish - I wait to hear her laugh and say, *"You came back for me. You remembered me."*

In that spirit of reverence and remembrance, I share *Gather*. *Gather* is a place to be human, to be imperfect, and to remember. May the words guide, nudge, whisper, or even shout you awake. May you hear the sound of my voice, now, as a woman unapologetically reclaiming her gifts and dreams. In these words, hear the voice of the little girl I had to remember in order to create *Gather*. May you hear your authentic voice.

Gather is not a book to be rushed or read from cover to cover.

Many of the insights within this book came to me during my Empowered Wisdom Yoga Nidra practice, meditation, or while giving myself permission to be easy and rest. After those experiences, I journaled, allowing whatever needed to be released into the pages of my journal to flow with no restrictions. No filter. No judgement. I organized the book in this same way for you —for you to read the short quotes and simply write what it means to you in the moment you encounter it. My meanings are on the back page following each quote. Another important part of my personal practice is self-inquiry. I've included questions that invite reflection and allow you to create an even more meaningful experience with *Gather*.

There's also another way to engage in the wisdom of this book.

Take a moment. Be quiet. Close your eyes. Breathe.

Allow your hands to touch the pages.

Turn to a random page and spend some time with the message. You may want to read the words aloud.

In whatever way you choose to use this book, my prayer is that you encounter a message that calls the scattered pieces within you back to wholeness.

I hope you gather and remember your Ancestors.

I hope you gather courage.

I hope you gather at your own heart.

I hope you rest in the gathering places you find throughout this book.

Octavia F. Raheem
November 2019

GATHER
ANCESTORS

When I put down what is not mine to carry,

I am free.

My mama's pain is not mine to carry. My daddy's suffering does not belong to me.

I don't have to make my grandmama's weariness my own to maintain a connection to her. I don't have to drink from the same cup of sorrow as my granddaddy to feel like we have something in common.

When I put down what is not mine to carry, I am free.

Free to face the very real, historic, and systemic oppression that created the suffering and pain for my people without the fear.

Free to access the power, courage, love, and strength of my lineage and carry it forward in a way that is boundless.

Free to command justice when and where I enter.

Free to call in peace with each breath.

Free to summon armies of protective guides to go before, behind, and surround me.

Free to pour the medicine of joy, harmony, and abundance from the ladle of my heart into the bowl of my being.

Free to drink deeply of the sweet nectar of my life.

Free to be at home wherever I am.

Free to walk a path of profound liberation with each step I take.

Free to rebuke the narrative that where and who I come from are permanently broken.

Free to remember how to rise and finally get on with the business of rising up.

Free to restore wholeness.

Free to stand and testify on behalf of myself and the millions who live within me: that my life matters. That our lives matter.

I've come to the place in my journey where it's time to release the pain and suffering of my Ancestors in order to access the freedom they prayed for me, my children, and their children to have.

My daily practice right now is to feel and release.

I do that through writing, Yoga Nidra, prayer, sacred movement, and self-love. I do this by being quiet enough to hear my heart and being brave enough to remember.

My Ancestors were more than pain and suffering.

So am I.

Name one gift you inherited (tangible or not) from your family? How do you share or express that gift in the world?

How much longer will you be too busy to fully enter into your own life?

Stick out your tongue.

Allow the infinite nectar of joy to drip there.

Nothing is in the void.

And so is everything.

The cosmic market is always open.

Will you keep circling the door?

How much longer will you be too busy to fully enter into your own life?

Will you keep passing your blessings by?

I know of a place.

We can go there and pause.

Let go.

Soften down.

Empty of conditioning,

We fill up with our truth.

In that place, our needs are already covered.

There, the only question is,

Beloved, what do you want?

Are you too busy to live, feel, and enjoy your life?

Be with your answer. If it needs to shift, what is one thing that you can do to change it?

When I nourish and take care of my body, I connect to the wisdom, power, courage, and love of my Ancestors.

What allowed my Ancestors to continue? What allowed them to hold on?

What kept them alive?

Despite everything that was set up against their humanity and survival,

What allowed them to hold on so that I could exist?

So that I could be here?

For years I've kept an Ancestral Altar, a sacred space to honor, remember, listen, speak to, nourish, and tend to the essence of my Ancestors.

Over the last year, and as my Empowered Wisdom Yoga Nidra practice deepens, I've come into the simple and profound awareness that my body holds the heart of my Ancestors. My blood is made of their blood. My body carries their reverent limbs. My eyes are deep portals to theirs.

My tongue carries their words, songs, prayers, and chants forward. My breath connects me to the place to which they have returned.

What I do to my body, I do to my Ancestors and to my future.

Reclaiming the inherent value in my Black and woman body requires me to confront messages, systems, and societal norms that tell me I am not worthy of my own care or love. It requires me to be deeply compassionate with myself as I come up against the ways I've internalized those negative messages.

Actively nourishing myself looks like-

sacred movement (sometimes that's asana), Yoga Nidra, home-cooked meals, resting, salt baths, drinking plenty of water, long deep hugs with people I love, using food grade oils on my skin, massage, or one of my sisters anointing my crown/doing my hair with holy oil and sweet grease.

Sometimes it's simply allowing myself space to be alone. To sit. To breathe.

No matter the medium, when I honor my body it is both an affirmation and an offering to my past, my Ancestors, my present, and my future.

I honor my body when I _____. *I promise to make time to* _____ *in order to connect to my Ancestors.*

We are human.

My Mama and I have messes. We have loudness. We have quiet. We've showed out on each other. We've shown up for each other. We've tried to change each other. We've transformed together. We've disagreed on almost everything. We've agreed on what really matters. We've let it all hang out and held a lot of it in. We've let space come between us. We've given each other space. We've taken space away from our relationship. We've refused to listen. We've heard. We've turned away from each other. We've never turned our backs on each other. We've let each other fall.

We've helped each other up every single time.

I celebrate my mama's imperfections and my own.

Love is patient, kind, and all sorts of things we have not always been. We are human.

We love each other, imperfectly.

Who do you love imperfectly? What I mean by this is you acknowledge that your relationship with them is evolving, a work in progress, and so worth it.

I have always been loved, wanted, and hoped for.

One of my beloved Ancestors met me in a dream.

She said she'd been waiting for me to visit and watching me.

She told me to sit down, listen, and look.

She needed to teach me something I couldn't access in books, lectures, sermons, or sanctuaries.

She said "Daughter, you got to pray with your whole soul, with your whole body, with your whole heart---most all the time out there. That's what I always been doin'."

I knew she was a Master of this medicine, prayer.

I also knew that her prayers made me.

I am woven together by threads of prayers spoken and whispered in her lifetime.

I have always been deeply loved, wanted, and hoped for.

I don't have to wait for anyone to grant me access to what is rightfully mine.

I do have to honor the principle of Sankofa- "go back and get it."

I have divine protection and guidance on my journey of reclamation and remembering that I come from love and so do you.

Asé, amen, glory, hallelujah.

Who has spoken into and over your life? Who has prayed for you? (still living or not)

Write a short note of gratitude to them.

I am held.

She is not smiling. Her arms are down, and her hands face me, palms wide open. I see all of her deep openings and the rivers that have woven through each wound and cracked place within her. Where the rivers merge, a pool of light radiates from within her. We face each other.

But why won't she smile at me? Am I not welcome? Does she not want to see me in this space? Am I taking too long to become? Is she impatient with my "hanging back" at the threshold? Are her palms open to push me across?

I want her to welcome me. To approve of my presence. To tell me I am good. That I made the right choices. To congratulate me on my ambition and drive. I am waiting for her to smile at me. Her smile will tell me all of those things. She looks at me.

I am skin. Bone. Vessels. And a fabric of sheer tissues in her presence. Her gaze goes clear through my body into my soul. She moves in closer to me. I see her eyes open into mirrors. She exhales. I soften. I feel her breath in my mouth.

And I realize, she is me.

She is me in our future. She is not smiling because she is waiting for me to honor all of my wisdom, to defy every condition and bond that no longer serves her, me, us. She is waiting for me to fully recognize that the light that I see in her is my own.

She is my future and my reflection.

I can stay hidden, small, and stuck. I can stand here and hold on to all of my stuff. It's heavy, yet so comfortable and known.

There is no way forward unless I put this shit down.

It takes a while. One by one, I let things go. One by one, I let go of the things. Her light allows me to see in the dark as I fumble through it all.

To surrender the conditions I've been clinging to so long that I've mistaken them for identity. To let go of ambition and ideas about "success." *Who am I without this armor? Those definitions? That mask? That costume? That belief?*

This is not easy. Weightlessness is uncomfortable when you've carried yours and everybody else's stuff for so long.

I lift my feet to cross the threshold. She offers her hand as compass and guide. Then, finally, she smiles.

The way forward is boundless when I let go. I am held.

What is your relationship to being held, being supported?

We are magic.

My namesake, my great-great paternal grandmama, Ms. Mama Octavia, was short, stubborn and didn't say anything she didn't mean.

The story goes she was released from a family she'd served when the grandfather of the family died. Along with her release, she was given the equivalent of pocket change to start her new life. She sewed that little bit of money up into a patch at the heart center of her dress and walked away without looking back.

The reality she was born into meant her time, space, and energy was claimed before she ever took her first breath. She needed to be stubborn. Tough.

My great-great grandmama shut down and locked up parts of herself to survive. I inherited those locks and that capacity to shut down as a means of survival. I have lived behind some of the closed-tight doors she had no choice except to hide within.

She refused to be broken. Her refusal to be broken kept her existence intact.

Because of her, I am here.

I inherited Ms. Mama Octavia's locks, and in this life, I've also inherited the keys. The prayers. The practices. The means to free up and manifest my fullest potential.

She continues to show up in my meditations, Yoga Nidra, and dreams. She continues to tell me:

"Daughter, the tools that aided our survival ain't always the same tools to thrive with. Open the locks, release the chains. You are meant to thrive."

My grandmamas are with me on every retreat. Every class. Every circle I hold space within.

They are as real as sunshine. They are mothers of magic. And so am I.

Write and repeat this to yourself at least seven times.

I am magic. I am magic. I am magic. I am magic. I am magic. I am magic. I am magic.

And then sit and breathe.

As I heal, I transform my lineage and legacy.

We can love our families of origin and also name the ways that we've been hurt by them. *Whew! That line was not easy to write.* My mama. Black. Woman. My daddy. Black. Man. Both had so much pressure and stress. So much unresolved trauma and pain-personal, familial, and systemic.

I understand that sometimes their best was muted and messy. Tangled up with fear, shame, rage, and too much pain.

The need to hold my mama and daddy safe and out of the claws of judgment is challenged by this season I am in. I am in a season of excavation. A season that demands that all that has been buried must be exhumed, examined, and released.

Where I come from, we don't air our dirty laundry. We scrub up real nice before anything is revealed. We are taught not to dig up old bones either.

Where I come from, we are misunderstood and misrepresented so often that we are careful not to add to it by talking too loud or too long about our dysfunction, our pain, our hurt, no matter where the infliction comes from.

I understand it, and perhaps you do as well.

And I can't honor that code anymore. At least, not within myself. I can no longer leave things stuffed up within me in order to "protect" someone else.

I have to look and feel, for myself, the impact and experiences of "their best," even when it was mangled and a misstep.

It's an act of immense love for self, my parents, and my family. It's a deeper devotion to examine and name our collective darkness. I know that all of those ways were learned, internalized, and passed on.

Which means they can be unlearned, released, and stopped.

As I heal, I transform my lineage and legacy.

I was conditioned to believe _____. *I am*
unlearning _____.

On behalf of our Highest Selves.

On behalf of our Ancestors.

Remember.

Remember who the EFF you are.

Make a list of all of the ways you radiate and shine.

Place it somewhere you'll remember to look every day.

As I heal, my Ancestors heal.

There are mamas in my blood. There are women who did not own themselves. So they could not claim their own children. They could not tend to their child. They could not feed their child from their own body if they wanted to.

I come from women who, for decades, were bound by systemic oppression that denied them the right to mother their children freely.

Caring for my son, feeding him from my body, choosing to work, for his laughter and my own, above and over the tears of the whole world, is the reclamation of what was stolen from those women who live through me.

Mothering is many, many things, and to be sure; it is complex. When my labor started, I prayed, "Heal the mamas in me, through me, in this delivery and in my mothering."

Both my pathway to Motherhood and my becoming a mother is soul and ancestral work.

I am not imprisoned by it. I am free to engage and express myself through it in ways that the mamas in my blood could not imagine.

My blood is theirs and a portal to our healing.

Write a prayer for healing for yourself and your lineage.

GATHER

COURAGE

You won't fit some places anymore. Grow anyway.

In my early 20's, I was in this relationship that stopped growing. It was comfortable. It was familiar. It was also going nowhere. It took me a minute of "stuckness" to decide to push back because I knew pushing was going to hurt. I knew it would create shifts within me that would require so much room that my only choice would be to leave and grow or stay and wither.

Ever been in a situation like that?

Afraid of outgrowing people and places that you've been "down" with for so long that you've shrunk yourself for days, weeks, maybe even years?

As a yoga student and teacher, the last 15 years have been full of growth spurts. My practice has changed. My style, too. My voice unearthed and has become less "polished" than when I started because the roots dangle off. Some shifts I've welcomed. I've resisted some of the transitions. All of them were essential to my wholeness.

I've outgrown places and people. People and places have outgrown me. It hurts.

Growing into my fuller self now, I realize some of my pains are feelings of wholeness returning to me as I rise after crouching down for so long.

Some will go.

Some will stay.

Grow. Grow anyway.

Complete this sentence: I am outgrowing _____.

I am growing into _____.

What does your YES feel like?

The quality of our YES matters.

When I make decisions from a place of empowerment and in the awareness that I have a choice, the energy of my YES is felt throughout the offering. Whether it is a mentorship, training, retreat, private lesson, or class, the YES is palpable and felt throughout.

So many times, we say YES out of fear, desperation, unworthiness, lack, to please people, or because we don't trust the power/love/ wisdom within our NO.

A YES made in fear colors the experience or offering a muted tone that feels half as vibrant as a bold no or real yes could feel.

I know what it is like to be in the presence of someone who is in the fullness of a YES moment. There's radiance. There's a profound sense of presence. I feel connected and held.

I know what a full YES feels like in my body. I also know that sometimes there are questions I need to be with before I access a clear answer, be it yes or no.

If what I am doing, saying, and offering is not an honest YES for me, how can it be experienced or received as a YES by anyone else?

What is a sure YES in your life right now? Name it.

Do not make someone else's mess your own.

The Lordt is continually working with me on this one. I backslide in my knowing from time to time.

It's like this though:

Folks who don't have, honor, or maintain their own boundaries have no capacity to respect yours.

They haven't built that inner muscle.

If we are not mindful, that lack of boundaries spills into interactions. It tries to become a force, banging up against your sanity, integrity, relationships. Your everything.

These days when I observe someone leaking and subconsciously or consciously offering me a handful of mess, I notice what's happening.

I bear witness and acknowledge what is actually going on without internally making anyone good, bad, worse, or better. I root down into my feet. I inhale/exhale with awareness at my heart.

I quietly say to myself, "I see you and all of that. I see you. And none of that leakage is mine or will become mine."

Or sometimes I simply say, and read this part out loud-

NAH.

Where do you need more boundaries in your life?

Do not shrink yourself.

Once upon a time, my asana practice was a place for me to deepen my dysfunctional relationship with my body versus love it. I used yoga to try and tame, fight, and mindlessly manipulate my body into a different shape or size.

I was practicing a form of self-harm under the guise of "wellness" for years.

I am so grateful for the teachers and spaces along the way that supported me in learning to honor my body/being in whatever shape or size it is in.

My yoga practice has revealed to me:

strength (inner and outer)

depth of compassion

how to honor my boundaries and other people's boundaries

the truth that can only be born from alignment

the power of stillness

how to move with intention

to acknowledge transitions and the spaces in between

the means to access the layers of my being that are folded within and yet even more expansive than my body.

Yoga has shown me how to stop trying to fit in, thus making myself small.

We are meant to grow.

What practices bring or keep you in good relationship with your body?

Today I affirm that every door that has been shut or slammed in my face was for my protection.

Today I know the most important door is the one to my own heart.

Through my yoga practice, through my self-effort, through my unwavering love for myself, family and community. Through my willingness to do my work. Through grace, the sacred door to my heart opens and expands.

Today I stand in this truth: the doors that matter, the doors that are mine to walk through, always open for me.

Have you ever had a door closed in your face? What opened as a result of it?

Growth is not linear and requires me to give up my stories.

Growth requires me to take bold action, speak my truth, and give over to grace - what my grit can't push me through. It is not linear and requires me to give up my stories, my clinging to limitations, even my own comfort in order for the seeds of my purpose to flourish into their fullest potential.

I am willing to give up _____ *in order for*
_____ *to grow in my life.*

Fire destroys. Fire creates. Both can be productive.

I am not the sparkly-eyed woman who dreamed of being a mama and studio owner anymore.

That woman crashed, burned, and dissolved into dust and ash.

And then I rose with a deeper luminescence in my eyes.

There is no way to see through the murky darkness of new beginnings and ancient endings unless your eyes adjust. They become the torch of fire that lights and guides your way through. If you've ever walked through corridors of darkness to get your baby. To get your dream. To gather your birthright that has been scattered in 1,000 pieces. To reclaim your purpose. If you've ever walked through hallways of darkness to take back what was yours, you know this:

Fire destroys. Fire purifies. Both are productive.

Do not be afraid of your fire.

Visualize yourself sitting in front of a fire. You are surrounded by guides, angels, and powerful forces of creation. You are safe. Breathe into your belly until you feel a sense of warmth there. What do you need to offer to the fire so that it can be destroyed and purified?

This moment, right now, is everything.

My partner put our son's "big boy" bed together while our son made us pancakes out of his sushi kit. I sat on the floor drinking a cup of tea.

I inhaled and sipped in the moment. I exhaled and let it nourish me and us. That moment became the best moment of my life because I was fully present for it.

I've always had incredible and tangible goals for each year. Today I don't have a goal I can touch. I am interested in total presence. In the simple sweetness within moments that often go by unnoticed.

Any moment where we fully show up has the potential to be the best moment of our lives.

I have right NOW.

This is the best moment of my life.

We have now. That's it.

I choose to show up to the life I have worked so hard for.

I want to linger in the love I conjured. To hold the family I prayed for. To enjoy the home we have created, together. To experience my studio as a student and let it be new and fresh in my heart that way.

This is the best moment of my life if I show up for it completely.

Nothing is worth more than right now.

Make a list of 5 things that bring you joy in your life right now.

The shortcut is the long way.

Sometimes it seems like her "glow up" happened overnight, or his "come up" was easy or breezy.

If we pull back the curtain on the person who inspires you, the person who you "love" and follow and "double tap like" on everything they post, it's likely you'll see plenty of failures, rejection, and mistakes.

You'll see resilience, self-effort, and challenging choices.

You'll also see a kind of discipline and devotion to their path that can't be reflected on a two-dimensional screen.

When I realized I wanted to teach yoga and create a sustainable wellness community by owning a yoga studio, I desperately wanted a shortcut.

I wasted time looking and wishing for one.

I haven't found a shortcut to my dreams that I would trust. I have discovered best practices that are rooted in integrity, relationships, and commitment to actually doing the work.

When I began teaching yoga, and I'd have 0-4 students in the class, I wanted to skip that part and hoped for some fast track way to fill my classes.

Thank goodness I never found it. I would have missed out on so many important and grounding lessons and relationships if it had happened any other way.

What process are you devoted to?

Your needs are valid.

What do you need? When was the last time you asked yourself that question?

Did you internalize that you should dismiss your needs, resent them, or deny them? Have you learned to hide them and have started to believe those "needs" make you weak or unlovable?

Maybe we've silently stayed in "relationships," intimate, work, or otherwise, where our needs are not acknowledged, honored, and met. The longer we allow "relationships" like that to prevail, the longer the narrative that our needs are not important, real, or worthy becomes within us.

What do you need in order to be your most brilliant and radiant self?

What do you need in order to do your work better and brighter?

What or who do you need to untangle yourself from so that your movements are freer?

Mamas, what do you need in order to honor your worth, work, and wisdom in your life, home, and the world?

What do you need in order to truly live?

Spend some time acknowledging your needs. Make a list. Have the conversations (inner and outer) you need to have about what you need to sustain your life.

And get ready.

Be willing to release whatever is within or outside of you that tries to diminish your connection to your essence and essentials.

Trust. Your needs are valid.

What do you have plenty of right now? What do you need more of?

What is for you cannot be taken.

It's a complex landscape out here. It is easy to slip and land in a place of covetousness. To get sidestepped and compare our actual work in real-time to someone else's virtual timeline. To cling so tight that we forget the simple truth that nothing can enter a closed hand.

The work I do is uncharted territory for me (and many). There is no blueprint, map, or GPS for how to get where I am going. I have to rely on my inner compass. The effectiveness of that compass depends on the clarity of my vision, my ability to see, at any given moment, a thing or person, including myself, for what it really is.

Grasping, comparing, and clinging are very human responses to living and working with the unknowns that come when we step out on our own and chart a fresh path. Yet, those things don't support more clarity. They crowd and cloud the windows of our minds, eyes, and hearts. In this way, it keeps us from fully seeing what we have, connecting to what we truly desire (vs. what we think we should want) and connecting to what is ours, and what belongs to us.

It also costs us energy that we could otherwise use to bring our full vision to fruition.

My mama used to say, "What God has for you is for you. Can't nobody fake it or take it."

When we bravely focus on our true path, we will see what is both present and in front of us. What belongs to us and what is real.

Everything else is a distraction.

Make a list of the top 5 ways that you distract yourself. Choose one and eliminate that distraction from your life for 7 days. Notice what happens.

You are worthy of your dream.

I can't put a price on my dream.

It does have a cost, though.

It cost me my addiction to grasping, lack, and limiting beliefs. It costed me comfortable, yet tired relationships and the capacity to maintain fake friends for status and social "mobility." It required me to pay in thousands of hours of teaching, studying, and learning totaling years and years before I left my day job. It cost me the familiarity of a time clock and the ability to delay responses like I did when I worked for someone else. I paid with misunderstandings and silent tears in rooms where I was the only Black yoga student or teacher.

All of these expenses have afforded me a sense of trust to know it's my birthright and responsibility to create and design a life that reflects the prayers of my mama and grandmama 'nem. It has netted me the capacity to discern the taste of an organic relationship in the making vs. a modified snack without nourishment on a plate filled with someone else's leftovers. It has granted me a level of integrity in my response and communication (time) with others who honor our potential or real-life relationships.

It has repaid me in understanding, smiles of soul recognition, and cries of release with yogis like and unlike me all over Atlanta, Georgia, and the Southeast.

Here I am free-er to be myself; to live, love, mother, create, and work on terms that my great-great grandmama might not have imagined.

Yes. It has cost me more than I have space to write in this book.

Yet, I owe no one more than I owe the girl I was, the woman I am, and the woman I am destined to become.

What do you really want? What does it cost? What are you willing to pay?

The woman you plan to become, be her now.

Long before I co-owned my yoga studio, I owned my work. I operated with the level of discipline, focus, commitment, care, and consistency that I believed owning a brick and mortar space would require. I was off by a lot *(owning a physical space asks for more than I could have ever imagined)*, yet the inner muscles I stretched and strengthened then expanded my capacity to both "hold down" and elevate the work I do now.

I honor the wise part of myself that knew that the kind of freedom I wanted required discipline.

I treated myself like the woman I hoped to be, and I grew into her.

I treat myself like the woman I am becoming. I continue to grow into her.

Being her now is

So much inner work.

Radical truth-telling.

Reshaping my most intimate relationships.

Defining my place vs. playing the role I was given.

It's not letting myself off the hook when it's hard.

It's lying down in soft places and praying more fervently than I ever have.

It's standing and walking through the fire until I see the blessing (tapas).

It's ugly crying to release the heat and cleanse.

It's bearing the gifts that my Ancestors gave without shame or apology.

It's trusting that what I've seen in my heart and mind's eye is mine.

It's the smallest of steps and decisions I make every day to be her now.

Sister, trust Her enough to do your work, now. Honor Her by tending to the details and process in the choices you make each day, right now. Let the distractions go.

No one else has read your book. She has. Every day that you sit down to write, you become the master of Her story.

No one has healed in your wellness space, yet. Every day that you save, plan, and study, so does she.

No one has walked the gardens you tend to. With every seed you dig and plant, your bare feet become more firmly rooted on Her true path.

No one has held the baby you long to carry. Mama, she has. With every layer of womb wound you peel back; she holds the baby.

No one has heard the songs you write except for Her. With each note and lyric you lay down, there's another track to carry Her forward.

Every step and stumble, you become more Her.

More of your whole Self.

---

*I am becoming*_____.

Look and see. The door is already open.

Should I ring or knock? Can I open the door? Should I go in?

There were years where I lingered at doorways.

For so long, I stood at the threshold between the stability, comfort, and predictability of my day job and the possibilities, unknowns, and what-ifs of working for myself or owning my own studio.

I shuffled at that threshold for some time. Preparing and preparing. Fretting and fretting.

Building. I learned how resourceful I am and how much a dream can really cost before you even meet it face to face. It will always cost more than you have saved in dollars and relationships. This year my business grew in ways I'd planned for, sweat out, cried about, and prayed for. It grew (or matured or expanded) in ways that signified the presence of pure grace. I allowed myself to feel worthy and deserving of it all. I crossed the threshold of "there's not enough" into "I am more than enough."

For years motherhood knocked on the door of my heart. I stood behind both sides of a double door. I was the one asking to enter and also the one whose hand could turn the key. I stood in front of a mirror distorted by conditioning, expectations, and even my own childhood. I straightened and re-straightened my clothes and life at that threshold. Afraid. I thought I had to line myself up perfectly before I could respond to the pounding at my own heart. I lingered and realized that as long as I saw my fear as an enemy, I couldn't learn from it and move forward.

I've been a mother for almost three years, and this year, I've more fully stepped into the love, challenge, fatigue, energy, softness, and strength of motherhood. I accept it as a great purpose and the most complex/beautiful door I've opened in my life.

The only way to see our way forward is to look straight ahead.

The only way to cross a threshold is to lift one foot, put it down, and then lift the other one.

Before you linger too much longer, knock, turn that key, or shake that knob.

Turn your gaze up. Turn your gaze as high as it can go.

Look and see.

The door is already open.

You belong inside.

What threshold is it time for you to cross?

GATHER

REST

Rest is fuel.

It seems so logical.

Me: I'm tired. Like I'm running on E.

Wisdom: Then rest. Chile rest. Rest, woman.

Me: When? After I check some emails, make another "to do" list, return some voicemails and...

Wisdom: Sweetheart. Now.

We can't drive a car on an empty tank, and most of us will head to the gas station and fill up as soon as we see that empty warning light come on.

Some of us might push it a few more miles, but we all know we have to fuel up at some point in order to get where we are going.

And sometimes we have reserves. That's the thing. Reserves should be used in an absolute crisis or emergency.

The best use of reserves isn't to post one more picture.

Do you use your reserves to send one more email?

When you are low on fuel do you still take one more appointment?

Do you push yourself to do one more load of laundry even when you are too tired to stand? Do you call in backup fuel to go out even though your body is begging to stay in? Do you have to say yes when we really deeply know the answer is hell nawl? These things are not crisis mode. These things don't actually require us to dig into our reserves, yet we do. We allow our fuel to be siphoned off little by little until we are empty.

What happens when we can't actually muster the energy to get on the path that belongs to us because we've used up so much of ourselves, our fuel, our reserves traveling a crowded highway, with folks, and toward places that we didn't really want to be on or with?

Rest fuels intuition.

Rest fuels better choices.

Rest fuels breath.

Rest fuels clarity.

Rest fuels patience.

Rest fuels creativity.

Rest fuels intimacy.

Rest is an honest fuel for our real journey.

When was the last time you reserved space and time to simply rest? Action: pull out your calendar and make a date to rest.

Invite in more ease.

What would it mean to approach even the hardest tasks with a spirit of ease?

What if we could trust more of our essence {who + whose we are} to support our greatest endeavors.

What if we pushed less? Could we create more? Could we become greater? Can we get a seat at the table if we work with more ease? If we make it to the proverbial table, can ease have a seat with us? What outdated belief system does straining support?

I am not suggesting that we dismiss our responsibilities.

Or that we don't respond or show up. That we don't get that 5:30 a.m. practice or workout in tomorrow. I am not suggesting that we call the whole thing off. That we shut completely down, even though sometimes that's what's required.

I am actually suggesting that we become more responsible, show up fuller. That we engage in a more complete way.

Pushing, pulling, straining, grasping, huffing, puffing, dreading, avoiding, distracting, but still managing to "get it all done" perpetuates more of itself. It's a self-sustaining, yet inefficient, and tired cycle.

If you have a mountain of work in front of you, breathe and pause. Drink water. Meditate. Face the mountain, clearly. Can you move through the mountain AND touch the grace of ease?

Looming deadlines? Drink some tea. Play your favorite song. Dance. Then give life to that deadline. Can you inspire a spark of ease in your process?

I've made an interesting turn in my journey. I can see backward and forward. I see how the energy, attitude, relentlessness in my grind is what got me where I am.

It. Has. All. Served. Me. Well.

And it is also not sustainable. To be clear, the discipline, the ethic, the responsiveness, is absolutely sustaining. My approach is not.

I am not looking for easy ways. I am inviting more ease into my work--more trust in my essence- the qualities that make me, me.

I am open to a place to lean more softly into the challenging, hard, and necessary prickly places of growth. Making friends with ease is a new relationship, and I can't resist the possibility it holds after a lifetime of grinding.

Are you friends with ease?

Rest is as necessary as breath.

Do you ever feel guilty when you rest? When you pause? When you don't answer the call? When you say no? When you slow down?

Where does that guilt come from?

For me, the guilt is textured, layered, and sometimes chain-like. It's from deep conditioning at an honest, ancestral level.

How much can you take? How fast? And with how little sustenance can you work? My Ancestors lived inside the systemic shackles of these questions and often died under their oppressive weight.

Add to that they lived the experience of working and doing, showing and proving TRIPLE times more than others for half a shot. You have the perfect conditioning to over-identify with work and assign your greatest personal value to that work. It's challenging even to trust rest when you've worn weary for so long. The heaviness of it has soaked through to your blood.

Resting is a practice of freedom for me and as necessary as breath. Rest allows my heart to remember a slower rhythm. It retrains my cells, blood, soul to trust that there can be rest for the weary. I rest for all of the women within me who never could.

Who taught you about rest as a form of self-care? What did they teach you? If you don't have an answer, write about how you plan to transform that legacy of not resting.

Slow down.

A while back, I was driving along in silence.

I heard a voice as clear as day. "Deer. Two. Ahead. Slow Down." I acknowledged the voice of warning, slowed down, and kept driving.

Ten minutes later, what did I see?

Deer.

Two.

I was grateful I'd heeded the warning and my pace had slowed considerably because one deer shot out into the road and stopped.

She stared at me. The other deer stayed off to the side of the road and watched. With intention, I pressed my brakes and stopped. I sat there, shoulders soft, face relaxed, and marveled at the beauty of both deer as they passed along.

Since I'd both heard AND honored the warning to "slow down," there was plenty of space to stop. The pause was easier than it would have been if I'd been speeding along.

My rational mind thinks, "Well, you live in Georgia. You know there are deer everywhere. No big deal. It makes sense to have a thought stick out in your mind to slow down at night in case you encounter deer." Yet, I know for sure there was something beyond rationality I heard speak to me that night.

I wonder if my mind had been crowded and jumbled up with "to do" lists as before, if I would have been able to hear such a clear message? Even if I would have been able to hear through the noise in my mind, would I have trusted the simple wisdom to slow down?

If I had been "so busy and rushing," would that deer and I have met a different fate?

Instead of pausing and seeing each other, would we have collided? Or at the least, would I have tensed up and been shaken at the sight of them versus taking in their beauty and waiting for them to pass?

That's the thing.

So much rushing leads to inner and outer collisions and to missing simple and beautiful moments.

Ever wonder what we miss because we can't hear the quiet and wise voice saying, "Slow down." Or we hear it, but we don't trust it or value it, so we decide to override the wisdom of that voice.

Are we too busy to slow down?

But not too busy to crash?

Pause. Take 5 slow breaths. Notice. What does that feel like?

Sometimes the next right step is to take a pause.

Sometimes the next right step is to put a knee down.

Sometimes it's to put both hands down.

Cause it's wobbly AF.

Sometimes it's to crawl.

Some moments the next right step is to turn off the phone.

Disable the messages.

Log off.

Sometimes the next right step is the complete sentence "No." The closing door.

Walking away without turning around.

It's saying "Yes" to your own space, time, and truth.

Sometimes the next right step is declining the offer that "no one could refuse."

It's being done with performing and the show vs. being authentic and real.

It's coming into alignment. It may not be big or flashy.

Right now, my next right step is only a breath. This one - inhale, pause, exhale, and pause.

Think of a challenge you are facing. What if the next right step is this-
simply pause (for a minute, an hour, or even a day?)

Self-love is an energy and action.

I am worthy of the time it takes to love

and nourish myself deeply.

Can you relate to this?

Let's say I'd commit to a three times a week practice starting on a Monday.

Day 1. Great! I practiced.

Day 2. Ok. Imma need to shorten my practice.

Day 3. Ummm...I'm too busy. My son oddly woke up too many times last night. Too many meetings today. Too many emails. I just can't deal.

Next week, the same thing. Except, now day two is looking like day three. A pattern forms and continues. Now weeks have turned into months.

I'd say something to myself like, "Don't beat yourself up for not practicing or doing that thing to nourish yourself. That's not kind. You don't need another thing to feel bad about."

Isn't the real "beating" staying in the cycle of not nourishing and honoring ourselves? Doesn't that further perpetuate "feeling bad" more than holding myself accountable for doing what I said I would do to fuel myself?

Here's the thing:

The "not kind" thing is ignoring our own needs.

The "not kind" thing is denying self the deeper breath.

The "not kind" thing is refusing to ask for support or help when we need it.

The "not kind" thing is allowing our boundaries to be so porous that our energy is continually leaking. (For me it's not resting or over-committing. And it's also something seemingly simple like not drinking enough water makes me feel porous.)

The "not kind" thing is running on 'E' and continuing to run.

Being kind to myself is:

Being brave enough to commit to myself and keeping those commitments.

This is brave because it requires staring down so much conditioning, so many systems and beliefs to honor self.

It's remembering and owning:

Self-love is an energy and action.

I am worthy of the time it takes to love and nourish myself deeply.

What does being more kind to yourself look like? Feel like? Sound like? Even taste like?

It's time to pause and listen.

I know how to run. I know how to move. I know how to hustle.

I know how to go hard. I know how to work. I know how to grind.

I know how to find a way or make one.

I know how to make a way. I know how to "tear da club up."

I know how to "eff it up." I know how to shut it down.

I know how to shout. I know how to cuss a mug out.

I know how to fight. I know how to hold on. I know how to wade in troubled water.

I know all of these things because I've had to know how to survive.

I want to survive, and I want to do so much more than survive.

I want to thrive. I want to grow. I want to expand.

I want to lay down things and folk that burden me.

I want abundance in love, time, energy, resources, space, joy.

I want to acknowledge the woman in me that shrugs and smugly asks, "Who are you to want more than your mama 'nem had?"

I want to see her and understand that she is no longer me.

It's so important to acknowledge what we've done when in survival mode.

To see the person within us who knew how to make it through the unspeakable.

And for the sake of our full selves, we must realize when we've reached a clearing.

When we can expand, even just a little.

It's important to notice when we no longer need to crouch down.

It's important to rise. It takes courage to shift a pattern that we've "rocked" for so long.

Abundance. The capacity and space to fully thrive is calling me.

I won't run. Move out the way. Cuss. Fight. Or otherwise, shut it down.

I know how to listen.

Being still and honoring quiet is how to be brave.

Now.

What pattern or habit supported you through some tough times yet no longer works for or serves you now?

You do not have to make decisions

when you are tired.

Listen:

You do not have to make decisions when you are tired.

You don't need to stall either.

Here's how I activate:

Rest

Yoga Nidra

Write

Get quiet

Pray on it.

Then decide.

Then make a move from a place of Empowered Wisdom.

I make the best decisions when I am _____.

It's okay to take a moment and connect with the most important person in your life. You.

It's hard to tell when we are disconnected from ourselves. When we are up to our ears in noise, we can't hear. When we are running from this place to that place to that. It's hard to discern the powerful messages coming at us and the ones arising from within us.

I connect to myself most deeply when I practice Yoga Nidra, restorative yoga, and write. These quiet practices invite me to stay close to the ear of my own heart and to tune into the messages within.

Remember what keeps you close to you.

Come back to that.

What practices and/or rituals allow you to maintain a connection to yourself?

Today has been prayed over.

I no longer wake up to the sound of the alarm of my household or business. I don't wake up, jump out of bed, and check email first either.

I get up before the sun. I engage the practices that allow me to sustain a sense of vision, devotion, and deep energy for my own healing, my family, my work.

I move/asana. I dry brush and self-massage (abhyanga).

I practice Empowered Wisdom Yoga Nidra.

I journal.

I pray.

I drink a cup of tea.

All of this most days before the sun rises.

I used to list the reasons I couldn't maintain a daily practice. The reasons I couldn't take care of my soul or Self. Some of them:

I'm a mama. I'm a business owner. Money. Time. Time. Time. Tired. I was always soooooo tired.

I heard myself listing those reasons one day and got curious about whether they were completely true or resistance?

If they were resistance, what was I resisting?

The short answer. Growth.

Why was I resisting growth?

Another short answer- It's uncomfortable. Nonlinear. Unknown.

My brand of soul/self-care doesn't cost much other than my relationship to the belief that I don't have time. It also cost me my attachment to the belief that I am not worth the time spent nurturing the soul of my being. The soul of me. Simply Octavia. The woman. No one else.

I don't crave sleeping in anymore. I want to be awake for my life.

Before I step into mothering, working, and loving everything and everybody else, I greet each day, knowing it has been prayed over.

What allows you to start your day with a sense of devotion?

It's time. Snatch your power back.

Grown women deserve space to dream. When we dream and vision, we remember and tap into our creative power.

Power.

Sisters, we have a wealth of creative power.

And for some of us, it's bound up, tied up, being poured out for everybody else, and leaking out in places where we lack boundaries in relationships, family, and work. It may be historical, but that's not our legacy.

It's time to snatch our power back.

Old paradigms and systems rely on women's complicity in being "drained" at home and work for its fuel. Abiding in that place won't create the space and time for you to dream and reconnect to your creative power.

Snatch your power back from the vampires, parasites, lazy lovers, energy drains, and inner gremlins that keep drinking up all the fuel you need to grow your visions and dreams.

Your family and even friends who depend on your energy to feed them and their visions and dreams even if it starves yours--- they may suddenly become unavailable or the opposite- clingy, as you begin "operation snatch back."

Gather your energy together anyway.

Snatch your creative power, your energy, and your fuel back. Run to the wide-open field of your own heart and mind. Dance freely in the field of your own imagination.

Rest and dream there. Your creative power is there.

Where are you leaking, losing, or giving away energy in a way that it's not being returned? How can you shift that one-sided energy exchange?

GATHER

ACKNOWLEDGEMENTS

You are holding this book because I have been held and supported
by so many-
seen and unseen.

To my Honorable Ancestors,
*Thank you for leaving me with hopes, dreams,
and a way to make a way.*

To my family of blood and water,
Jemar Raheem, Oyetunde Raheem, Millie Miller, Ebony, Mario,
Kamyrn, and Ariana Reynolds, Angela, Ladawn, and Abanu
Strickland

Thank you for being both roots and wings.

Deep bow at the feet of my Beloved Teachers,
Tracee Stanley, Chanti Tacoronte-Perez
Dr. Gail Parker, Maya Breuer, Graham Fowler, and Gina Minyard

*Thank you for holding up your Light
for me to find, see, and reclaim my own.*

To my circle of sisters,
Starshine & Clay , Held Mentor Group, Sacred Chill West Family
Yoga, Literature, and Art Camp For Teen Girls

Thank you for keeping me lifted in prayer, laughter, and truth.

To Brook Blander,
Thank you for being my editor, designer, and so much more.
Thank you for insisting I take more time to honor the way *Gather*
wanted to be born. A way that was not on my timeline, but
something more Divine.
Thank you for gathering me and showing me another way.
Thank you for walking with me all of the way home.

ABOUT THE AUTHOR

Octavia Faith Ann Raheem is a mother, writer, and yoga teacher. She grew up in Gainesville, Georgia, a place that will forever soak her roots in red clay.

She is the co-owner of Sacred Chill {West} in Atlanta, Georgia. She is also the founder of Starshine & Clay Yoga Retreats for Women of Color and Held Mentor program for yoga teachers and wellness workers.

She has many dreams and is doing her best to write, speak, see, and touch them all.

She shares her thoughts and works on her website www.octaviaraheem.com as well as Instagram: @octaviaraheem.

GATHER

GATHER YOURSELF

Made in the USA
Middletown, DE
06 September 2024

59921131R00080